CONTENTS

PREFACE

Economic analysis typically attributes differences in corporate social responsibility (CSR) between firms to either, 1) differences in beliefs concerning what companies *should* do, or 2) differences in the 'objective' situations faced by firms. Whether firm leaders should take a 'morally neutral'/instrumental view of stakeholders, or take an intrinsic view of stakeholders guided by a 'moral compass,' is generally viewed as an exclusively normative issue. Given the assumptions concerning individual and firm behavior from traditional economic theory, the instrumental and morally neutral perspective wins unequivocally leaving situational characteristics such as firm size, industry dynamics, and the ability to differentiate products as the only causes for the observed differences in CSR between firms that are explored.

The neoclassical behavioral model views people as exclusively self-regarding, and generally assumes that different individuals would make the same assessment of a given situation. These strict assumptions are inadequate for examining why different firms implement different levels of CSR. Significant uncertainty exists when evaluating most any investment. Even if faced with the same circumstances, bounded rationality and selective perception cause decision makers to use different assumptions in identifying and estimating investment costs and benefits. One of the key assumptions impacting the profitable level of CSR relates to the beliefs about human behavior and how stakeholders will respond to firm actions. Specifically, a decision maker who believes people are predominately self-interested will estimate smaller financial benefits to the firm from proactive CSR than a decision maker who believes people are significantly cooperative, other-regarding and social.

Recognizing these issues opens the possibility that the arguments typically labeled as purely normative can be strategic as well. An instrumental treatment of stakeholders can only be equated to *the* strategic view when human behavior is believed to be reasonably described by Homo economicus. However, if a behavioral model inspired by psychology and sociology is used, such as the one in Stewardship Theory or Servant Leadership Theory, the equality of instrumental and strategic does not necessarily hold, and an intrinsic treatment of stakeholders may paradoxically be the better strategic choice. Each of these points is examined in detail.

Chapter 1

INTRODUCTION

ALTRUISM IN ECONOMICS

Mesmerized by Homo economicus, who acts solely on egoism, economists
shy away from altruism almost comically. [Samuelson 1993, p. 143]

In evolutionary biology an altruistic act is one where an organism engages in
behavior that benefits the reproductive fitness of another organism, at a cost to its
own reproductive fitness. There is no motivational assessment required in
satisfying this definition. In contrast, economic analysis generally uses a
definition for altruism that requires an explicit motivational criterion, in addition
to an outcome criterion, to be met for an action or individual is labeled altruistic.
Some example definitions include:

- The altruist is someone who is affected by the level of welfare enjoyed by
  (at least some) others and is moved to act on their behalf. [Miller 1988, p.
  165]
- I describe individuals as altruistic when they feel and act as if the welfare
  of others were an end in itself; that is, as something of relevance
  independently of its effects on their own well-being. [Zamagni 1995, p.
  xv]
- Altruism is the preference for the good of some other people in itself, and
  it also denotes acting in favour of this good for this motive. [Kohm 2006,
  p. 19]

As indicated by the opening quote by Samuelson, altruism is even more typically avoided in economic analysis or explained away as an irrational anomaly [Manner and Gowdy, 2009].

Many economists might suggest that what is called altruism is, in fact, self-interested behavior where individuals have merely expanded their utility functions to include the utility functions of others rather than only 'own' income. What is called pure altruism may be motivated by the good feeling, satisfaction, or health benefits one receives from seeing a cause advanced that is considered by the individual to be worthy. The problem is, as Fehr and Schmidt [1999, p. 817] state: "Almost all economic models assume that *all* people are *exclusively* pursuing their material self-interest and do not care about "social" goals per se." However, in an attempt to avoid a theoretical debate as to the nature of or existence of altruistic motives, the term altruism will not generally be used in this chapter. Instead, less contestable terms such as other-regarding, pro-social and cooperative will be used to describe individual and firm preferences for pro-active corporate social responsibility. Although many may debate the idea of CSR as an act of altruism, most will hopefully agree that a desire for it reflects pro-social and other-regarding preferences and/or behavior.

CORPORATE SOCIAL RESPONSIBILITY DEFINED

The breath of possible definitions for the corporate social responsibility (CSR) construct requires any discussion to explicitly clarify the definition being used. Without this clarification any statements or assertions are vulnerable to confusion, with the reader's definition of CSR guiding the interpretation [McWilliams et al., 2006]. For the purposes here, corporate social responsibility [CSR] will be defined as:

Actions that appear to further some social good, beyond the interests of the firm and that which is required by law. [McWilliams and Siegel 2001, p. 117]

This definition seems to capture the essence of what the majority of practitioners exploring the area, and the majority of the business community consider CSR. Most suggest that there must be benefits beyond legal requirements [Davis 1973; Vogel 2005]. Here, 'beyond the interests of the firm' is interpreted as representing benefits besides profits to shareholders. The extensive debate and research concerning whether CSR is or is not profitable indicates that most do not define CSR as only those initiatives that are *beyond* profits, but that it includes both profitable and unprofitable initiatives that have social benefits. It should be noted that this view is not universal, with some suggesting it is only includes those actions beyond profits [Frank, 2004; Kolstad, 2007; Klonoski, 1991; Reinhardt et al. 2008], some suggesting that profitable actions are the only socially responsible actions [Friedman, 1970] [1], and some suggesting it doesn't make sense to talk about social responsibilities separately from financial responsibilities [Harrison and Freeman, 1999]. Many of arguments behind these alternative views have merit but also challenges. For example, using "sacrificing profits in the social interest" [Reinhardt et al. 2008, p. 219] as the definition of CSR would suggest that a firm implementing a carbon neutral production process, that has a profit neutral impact, would not increase the firm's corporate social performance. However, the spirit behind the view of Harrison and Freeman [1999] is reflected in some of the ideas asserted in this chapter.

---

1 Friedman [1970] actually suggests that the existence of the CSR concept is troublesome in and of itself.

Chapter 2

THE NORMATIVE DIVIDE

The debate concerning the level of CSR the firm, and its leaders, *should* implement often frames the issue as a battle between two polar normative views. On one side are those who argue for profit maximization, an instrumental perspective toward non-owner stakeholders (hereafter simply referred to as stakeholders), and a 'morality neutral' perspective from firm leaders when making decisions on behalf of the firm. On the other side are those who argue for broader firm goals than only profits, an intrinsic view of stakeholders, and the use of a 'moral compass' by decision makers. The next several sub-sections provide an overview of these seemingly opposing positions.

STAKEHOLDER THEORY: WIDELY USED BUT NORMATIVELY DIVIDED

Freeman's [1984, p. 46] seminal book, 'Strategic Management: A Stakeholder Approach' defines modern stakeholder theory, and provides the following well known definition:

> A stakeholder in an organization is [by definition] any group or individual who *can affect or is affected by* the achievement of the organization's objectives.

McWilliams and Siegel [2001] suggest that stakeholder theory is the most widely used perspective from which to examine CSR, and it is the main perspective used in this dissertation. Mitchell et al. [1997, p. 880] suggest that "Stakeholder theory, we believe, holds the key to more effective management and to a more useful, comprehensive theory of the firm in society." They propose a theory of stakeholder identification and salience based upon who managers *should* [to achieve certain ends] pay attention to. This is defined by whether a potential stakeholder possesses one or more of the following attributes; 1) power to influence the firm, 2) legitimacy of their relationship with the firm, and 3) urgency of their claim on the firm.

Although there does not seem to be a tremendous amount of debate with the general definition of a stakeholder, there is a tremendous amount of debate as to *what ends* managers should use in deciding which of these attributes are relevant to decisions of the firm, and how to apply them. Berman et al. [1999, p. 488] suggest that the two models of stakeholder management that are most typically used are, a "strategic stakeholder management model" and an "intrinsic stakeholder commitment model." A strategic approach is generally attributed to the profit maximization perspective, with the financial implications to the firm as the only reason for considering the interests of stakeholders [Berman et al., 1999]. An intrinsic stakeholder approach is generally attributed to an alternative normative view that treats stakeholder interests as an ends in themselves rather than only as a means to profits. This description of the intrinsic stakeholder approach directly relates to the definition of altruism from Zamagni [1995] provided earlier.

Freeman [1984] defines something with intrinsic value as good in and of itself, and which is to be pursed on its own account and worth. In contract, things with instrumental value only have value because they contribute to the achievement of something with intrinsic value. Berman et al. [1999, p. 491] suggest that under the intrinsic stakeholder commitment model, "....if stakeholders are affected by the achievement of the firm's objectives, it follows that the firm's decisions affect the well-being of its stakeholders, which in turn suggests the possibility of a normative obligation to stakeholders on the firm's part." They describe this motivation as, "...managers feeling they have a fundamental moral obligation to stakeholders that grounds their managerial approach." Decisions are guided by fundamental principles that explicitly consider stakeholder interests to help define what the company stands for [Berman et al., 1999].

Using the framework developed by Mitchell et al. [1997] it can be generally concluded that those arguing for the strategic stakeholder management model consider the only relevant power relationship being when stakeholders have power to impact the financial performance and/or operations of the firm. In contrast, those arguing for the intrinsic stakeholder commitment model generally consider stakeholder power to impact the firm *and* firm power impact the stakeholder as relevant [Freeman and Liedtka, 1991]. For the strategic model, the legitimacy attribute is typically defined in legal [contractual] and economic terms only, whereas for the intrinsic model generally also includes a moral component. Those arguing for the strategic stakeholder view, with non-shareholder stakeholders considered to have instrumental value only, generally seem to view the firm more as a private institution [Jensen and Meckling, 1976]. Those arguing for the intrinsic view generally seem to view the firm more as a social institution [Waddock et al., 2002]. The debate between these views is typically framed in exclusively normative terms, with those who argue that firms should maximize profits on the instrumental side, and those who suggest that firms need to consider other goals and issues in addition to profits on the intrinsic side. There are other variations on these themes, however, most seem to effectively be debating whether firms should or should not *focus exclusively on profits*, and normatively why they should or should not. Given the assumptions concerning individual and firm behavior from standard economic theory, the profit/instrumental/morally neutral perspectives win unequivocally over the assumed strategically inferior intrinsic view of stakeholders, where decisions of firm leaders are guided by a moral compass.

CSR: THE FIRM AS A SOCIAL INSTITUTION

Grown to tremendous proportions, there may be said to have evolved a "corporate system"--as there was once a feudal system--which has attracted to itself a combination of attributes and powers, and has attained a degree of prominence entitling it to be dealt with as a major social institution. [Berle and Means 1933, p. 1]

Standard economic theory, and the exclusive fiduciary responsibility it gives to shareholders, views business as fundamentally a private enterprise. Under this view management has an exclusive fiduciary responsibility to shareholders, and any responsibility toward other stakeholders is derived only in the extent they advance shareholder interests. Many, however, view the corporation as a social institution that relies on society for the ultimate legitimacy of its existence. Under this view, profit seeking is often portrayed as a benefit provided by society in the unofficial corporate charter of social norms, where the needs and desires of society shape the expectations on business firms:

It is reasoned that the institution of business exists only because it performs valuable services for society. Society gave business its charter to exist, and that charter could be amended or revoked at any time that business fails to live up to society's expectations. Therefore, if business wishes to retain its present social role and social power, it must respond to society's needs and give society what it wants. [Davis 1973, p. 314]

Wood [1991, p. 695] suggests, "The basic idea of corporate social responsibility is that business and society are interwoven rather than distinct entities; therefore, society has certain expectations for appropriate business behavior and outcomes." Gowdy [2005a] suggests that the idea that firms and markets are socially constructed is nothing new. It has been advanced by Marx, Veblen, Weber, Galbraith and many others before and since. Berle and Means provide a justification for this assertion based upon the fundamental changes to the concept of business as private property with the separation of ownership and control:

> On the one hand, the owners of passive property, by surrendering control and responsibility over the active property, have surrendered the right that the corporation should be operated in their sole interest,--they have released the community from the obligation to protect them to the full extent implied in the doctrine of strict property rights....Eliminating the sole interest of the passive owner, however, does not necessarily lay a basis for the alternative claim that the new powers should be used in the interest of the controlling groups. The latter have not presented, in acts or words any acceptable defense of the proposition that these powers should be so used. No tradition supports that proposition. The control groups have, rather, cleared the way for the claims of a group far wider than either the owners or the control. They have placed the community in a position to demand that the modern corporation serve not alone the owners or the control but all society. [Berle and Means 1933, p. 355]

Ghoshal [2005, p. 79] suggests the same:

> After all, we know that shareholders do not own the company--not in the sense that they own their homes or their cars. They merely own a right to the residual cash flows of the company, which is not at all the same thing as owning the company....Indeed; it is this fundamental separation between ownership of stocks and ownership of the assets, resources, and the associated liabilities of a company that distinguishes public corporations from proprietorships or partnerships. The notion of actual ownership of the company is simply not compatible with the responsibility avoidance of "limited liability."

The view of firms as social institutions suggests that CSR initiatives be evaluated not only on their costs and benefits to the firm, but also on the impact these initiatives have on society. This suggests an identification of relevant stakeholders that includes those *affected by* the firm, not only those who can affect the profits of the firm. Freeman and Liedtka 1991, p. 95] suggest that, "Creating the good society will require that the business community accept a new set of moral imperatives." This last point highlights how the view of business as a social institution often suggests an intrinsic view of stakeholders and a treatment of them that is guided by a moral compass.

CSR AND PROFIT MAXIMIZATION: THE THEORY OF THE FIRM PERSPECTIVE

Those examining CSR from a theory of the firm perspective dismiss most arguments for viewing firms as social institutions as normatively based and misguided. Only to the extent that business legitimacy constraints can *clearly* be demonstrated to impact profits do they become relevant to the analysis [Waldman and Siegel 2008]. Significant academic work has debated whether CSR is profitable or not, with some concluding it is [Waddock and Graves, 1997], some finding it is not [Wright and Ferris, 1997], and some finding or suggesting a neutral relationship [McGuire et al., 1988; McWilliams and Siegel 2000; 2001]. Using a theory of the firm perspective, McWilliams and Siegel [2001] hypothesize that there is a level of CSR that is in line with profit maximization, and that studies finding a positive relationship between a firms' proactive engagement in CSR and profitability may do so as the result of model misspecifications [McWilliams and Siegel, 2000]. They suggest firms should treat CSR "precisely as they treat all investment decisions" and that, "there is an "ideal" level of CSR, which managers can determine via cost-benefit analysis, and that there is a neutral relationship between CSR and financial performance" [McWilliams and Siegel 2000, p. 117]. For example, Shrivastava [1995, p. 955] suggests that companies such as Dow Chemical and Tokyo Electric Power Company, "routinely make ecological investments as part of their capital-investment programs." Although in a meta analysis of studies Orlitzky et al. [2003, p. 427] find that, "corporate virtue in the form of social responsibility and, to a lesser extent, environmental responsibility is likely to pay," their analysis and a subsequent follow-up discussion [Orlitzky, 2008] do not seem to completely refute the possibility that misspecification creates the overall positive, rather than positive up until some point, conclusions of McWilliams and Siegel. This concept is well articulated by Kolstad [2007, p. 143]:

> From a theoretical point of view, the position that CSR always increases profits is quite easily refuted. Certainly, a company may get a reputation boost by doing some kind of socially beneficial work that goes beyond its normal operations. But after the initial boost, a company will not get as much of an effect if it further expands its CSR activities. At some point, the costs of expanding CSR activities will outweigh the benefits to the company.

Initiatives that have been suggested as having possible profit benefits include, non-animal testing, recycling, abating pollution, supporting local businesses and embodying products with social attributes or characteristics such as being pesticide or dolphin free [McWilliams and Siegel, 2001]. Berman et al [1999, p. 489] summarize the following ways in which profit motivated firms can improve the natural environment:

> First, being proactive on environmental issues can lower the costs of complying with present and future environmental regulations. Second, environmental responsiveness can enhance firm efficiencies and drive down operating costs. Third, firms can create distinctive, "eco-friendly" products that appeal to customers, thereby creating a competitive advantage for the firms. Fourth, being environmentally proactive not only avoids the costs of negative reactions on the part of key stakeholders, but can also improve a firm's image and enhance the loyalty of such key stakeholders as customers, employees, and government.

Another example relates to philanthropic acts by the firm that are valued sufficiently by current or potential customers, such that engaging in this activity increases profits by more than enough to offset the cost. For example, donations to the Dallas Symphony Orchestra by Southwest Airlines, whose headquarters and largest base are in Dallas, may sufficiently increase customer loyalty and demand to more than offset the expense of the donations. Godfrey and Hatch [2007, p. 88] suggest that this type of "strategic philanthropy" results in, "a balance sheet effect through which firms build loyalty, legitimacy, trust and brand equity." It is effectively a brand building, advertising expenditure for Southwest that has social benefits, but is also expected to be profit enhancing for the firm. Other examples include a marketing benefit from sponsoring community sports teams [Panapanaan et. al., 2003] and assumed quality advantages by customers for firms engaging in proactive CSR [McWilliams and Siegel, 2000].

For many firms in many situations one of the most significant advantages relates to the positive impacts on employees. A proactive engagement in CSR often improves worker loyalty, and increases the ability to attract recruits [McWilliams and Siegel 2001; Berman et al., 1997]. If CSR initiatives are incorporated into 'what we are' and 'what we stand for' as a company, they can help create a shared sense of purpose that Ghoshal and Moran [1996] suggest produces significant advantages for the firm. This inspired sense of purpose may not only increase loyalty and productivity, but may spur creativity and innovation as well. Husted and Salazar [2006] suggest that economic programs that relate directly to the firms strategy and mission are most likely to be profitable.

McWilliams and Siegel [2001] suggest that the profit maximizing level of CSR demanded by stakeholder groups will be higher; the more profitable the industry, the larger the firm, the more diversified the firm, with experience versus search goods, for higher levels of income of the customer base, under tighter labor market conditions, with the ability to differentiate its products, among other factors. From this, they suggest that RandD spending and advertising intensity are strategic variables chosen by the firm that can be used to help predict the CSR levels:

....firms pursuing product differentiation/image/reputation building strategies will have an incentive to be socially responsible. [Waldman, Siegel and Javidan 2006, p. 1704].

Husted and Salazar [2006, p. 76] provide a marginal cost and marginal benefit framework that they use in, "examining conditions under which profit maximization and social performance are congruent." Their graphical framework is reproduced in Figure 1. The x axis represents the positive social impacts of the company (which they call social output). The total costs and benefits of CSR initiatives are represented by the Cost Curve and Benefit Curve respectively. Consistent with standard economic marginal analysis, the level of social output is selected where the marginal cost and marginal benefit of the next dollar spent on the initiative are equal. This occurs at the level of social output (represented by X_{s1*}) where the slope of the benefits curve (the marginal benefit) is equal to the slope of the marginal cost curve.

The authors suggest that, if a firm designs their CSR strategy *for the purpose of* capturing the types of benefits described in the preceding paragraphs, it can actually raise the firm's benefits curve and/or lower the firms cost curve. This result is proposed to occur due to the creation of synchronistic effects (ex. improve energy efficiency while simultaneously being perceived as a 'green' company). This type of effect is represented in figure 3.1 by the higher strategic benefit curve and/or lower strategic cost curve, with the result of raising the profit maximizing level of social output to X_{s2*}. The shifts are more likely, "when such programmes are central to the firm mission, highly specific, proactive, visible, and voluntary" [Husted and Salazar 2006, p. 82]. They give examples such as, revenue benefits from the ability to differentiate products, reduction in costs due to improvements in energy efficiency, avoidance of negative or increase in positive government interventions (ex. environmental regulations and tax breaks respectively), and improvements in reputation. The reputation effect potentially creates benefits such as, the ability to attract, retain and motivate higher quality employees. This last benefit in particular, is generally extremely hard to measure and quantify.

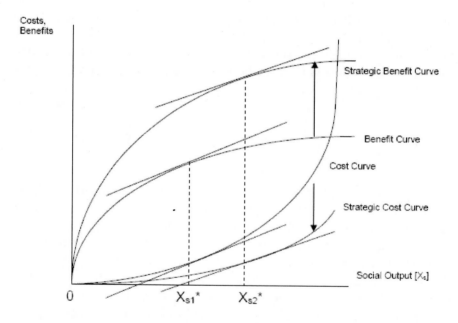

Figure 1. Benefits of Strategic CSR.

Husted and Salazar [2006, p. 76] conclude:

> It is wiser for the firm to act strategically than to be coerced into making investments in corporate social responsibility. In addition, we argue that greater overall social output will be achieved by the strategic approach, than by the altruistic approach.

This conclusion is based on the assumption that the benefit curve does not shift up, and the cost curve does not shift down for either a firm that, a) takes a reactive stance toward CSR, where they participate only if coerced into doing so, or b) takes an altruistic stance, since the authors assume that the altruistic firm, "has neither the intention nor the motivation to shift these curves" [Husted and Salazar 2006, p. 86]. Their analysis is consistent with the theory of the firm perspective and leads to the conclusion that a purely instrumental approach to stakeholders is required in order to identify this profit maximizing point.

Chapter 3

UNCERTAINTY, BOUNDED RATIONALITY AND BEHAVIORAL ASSUMPTIONS

> In the face of future uncertainty, the profit-maximizing motive does not provide the entrepreneur with a single and unequivocal criterion for selecting one policy from among the alternatives open to him. [Enke 1951, p. 567]

Economic analysis often abstracts from the inherent uncertainty involved in estimating the costs and benefits of potential investments. This is done through the assumptions of human behavior in economic analysis:

> The economic approach basically starts from two related, untenable assumptions concerning the nature of human behavior: [i] economic agents behave according to the normative rational model, and [ii] every economic agent acts, ceteris paribus, in the same way. [Boone et al. 1999, p. 344]

The authors refer to this second assumption as "homo anonymous," which effectively results in the differences between the assumptions used by individuals when faced with uncertainty being ignored. This abstraction through assumptions can be seen in the papers by McWilliams and Siegel [2000; 2001]. These papers contribute much to the analysis of firm investments in CSR that can be useful to both academics and firm managers in identifying factors that are likely to impact the demand for CSR of firms *facing different situations*. However, by suggesting that, "managers can use this framework to determine *precisely* [emphasis added] how much they should spend on CSR" [McWilliams and Siegel 2001, p. 119] the authors focus exclusively on the situational differences and ignore the uncertainty involved for the decision maker in actually estimating the costs and benefits. Similarly, Husted and Salazar [2006] only examine differences in costs and benefits due to firms defining *different ultimate goals* for their CSR investment strategies. Their strategic perspective still uses the "homo anonymous" and normative rationality assumptions to abstract from decision maker uncertainty in determining the most profitable combination of investments.

Cyert and March [1963[1992], p. 9] summarize the implications of these assumptions on the analysis of the firm:

> The "firm" of the theory of the firm has few of the characteristics we have come to identify with actual business firms. It has no complex organization, no problems of control, no standard operating procedures, no budget, no controller, no aspiring "middle management." To some economists it has seemed implausible that a theory of an organization can ignore the fact that it is one.

They go on to suggest that the theory of the firm is really a theory of markets, and is not designed to handle the internal allocation of resources within a firm. Others have made similar assessments about the theory of the firm [Williamson, 1981; Jensen and Meckling 1976]. Simon [1979, p. 494] criticizes, "the rather weak and backward development of the descriptive theory of decision making including the theory of the firm" from economics. He suggests that Friedman appears to believe that, "fundamental inquiry into rational human behavior in the context of business organizations is simply not [by definition] economics." He points out the ironic discrepancy of this view:

> Thus economists who are zealous in insisting that economic actors maximize turn around and become satisficers when the evaluation of their own theories is concerned. [Simon 1979, p. 494]

As with all economic analyses, simplifications need to be made to be able to say much of anything. In examining the general directional influences of situational factors on demand for CSR [McWilliams and Siegel, 2001], or for proposing the general implications of fundamentally different goal perspectives on the profitability of CSR [Husted and Salazar 2006], the assumption of "homo anonymous" may make sense. However, recognizing that decision uncertainty remains after the situational influences are considered, transforms the proposed precise determination of how much should be spent on CSR into the more realistic directional predictions or shifts in the reasonable range of estimates. March and Simon [1991, p. 138] points out that with certainty, the choice is obvious, with risk: pick the highest expected value, but with uncertainty, "The definition of rationality becomes problematic."

Simon [1979] suggests that a strong positive case for replacing the classical theory by a model of bounded rationality begins to emerge when we examine situations involving decision making under uncertainty and imperfect competition. "These situations the classical theory was never designed to handle, and has never handled satisfactorily" [Simon 1979, p. 497]. He goes on to suggest that the classical model provides little help as management decision rules: "For these domains, idealized models of optimizing entrepreneurs, equipped with complete certainty about the world—or, at worst, having full probability distributions for uncertain events—are of little use." Bertrand and Schoar [2003] find that managers vary significantly in their decision making, even under seemingly very similar circumstances. Wide experiences in public accounting, management of a major airline and in consulting to large and small firms have provided me with countless examples that support this conclusion.

The recognition of this decision uncertainty opens for discussion the question at hand: 'What affects how different decision makers evaluate the costs and benefits of a particular CSR initiative in a particular industry/firm situation?' As theoretical economic analysis generally abstracts from this question by, a) only looking at direction of change and ignoring magnitude, and b) assuming that all economic agents act in the same way when faced with the same situation, different behavioral assumptions are needed. Economists generally don't like to broach these issues. As Kahneman et al. [1986b, p. S299] suggest, "adding complexity to the model of the agent generally makes it more difficult to derive unequivocal predictions of behavior from a specification of the environment." Many suggest that this is the most important reason economists cling to these assumptions. However, differences in individual behavior clearly exist that are important for examining the current issue:

> Taken together, our findings clearly show that individuals behave strikingly differently although confronted with exactly the same [market] situation. [Boone et al. 1999, p. 367]

This uncertainty, at the very least, leaves a wide range of *justifiable* (from an expected long term financial performance perspective) CSR investment levels for firm leaders to follow in any particular situation. When attempting to examine the behavior of individual firms, and the managers within them, an abstraction from this form of decision uncertainty leaves little to examine.

Bounded Rationality and Selective Perception

> It is sometimes useful to enrich the model of economic agents by explicitly introducing a behavioral factor that is ignored in the standard theory. Such an effort is ultimately tested by whether it helps to resolve recognized anomalies and to identify new ones. [Kahneman et al. 1986b, p. S299]

Hambrick and Mason [1984, p. 194] suggest that "bounded rationality, multiple and conflicting goals, myriad options, and varying aspiration levels all serve to limit the extent to which complex decisions can be made on a techno-economic basis" and that "complex decisions are largely the outcome of behavioral factors rather than a mechanical quest for economic optimization." Under this view, the decision maker brings a cognitive base and values to a decision, which creates a filter between the situation and his or her perception of it:

> The manager's eventual perception of the situation combines with his/her values to provide a basis for strategic choice. [Hambrick and Mason 1984, p. 195]

Hambrick [2007, p. 337] proposes that executives' experiences, values, and personalities, "affect their, (1) field of vision (the directions they look and listen), (2) selective perception (what they actually see and hear), and (3) interpretation (how they attach meaning to what they see and hear)." Given this dynamic, the same objective situation is seen differently, and results in different decisions from different individuals [Thomas and Simerly, 1994]. Boone et al. [1999, p. 345] suggest that although, "the importance of individual differences as determinants of behavior has long been recognized by psychologists" these differences are not generally reflected in economic analysis.

Different Goals or Different Assumptions

> When such divergent results are obtained by the application of the logic of two major social disciplines to a new fact situation, we must push our inquiry still further back into the assumptions and concepts of those disciplines. [Berle and Means 1933, p. 345]

As described earlier, the debates between the intrinsic and instrumental view of stakeholders, and between the theory of the firm perspective and the firm as a social institution, are often portrayed as representing opposite or polar normative viewpoints concerning, whether; a firm should [Friedman, 1970] or should not [Berle and Means, 1933] focus exclusively on maximizing profits; firm leaders do [Jensen and Meckling, 1972], or do not [Simon, 1987; Berle and Means, 1933] have an exclusive fiduciary responsibility to shareholders; the efficiency goal of firms does [Williamson, 1981], or does not [Gowdy, 2005a] best promote societal well-being; the business firm is primarily a private institution [Williamson, 1981] or a social institution [Wood, 1991]. Although sometimes these questions are central to the debate, often the underlying differences seem to be less a matter of different goals (profits or not), than a matter of different beliefs and assumptions; particularly the assumptions concerning human behavior.

An exclusive focus on the normative question ignores the variation that can exist between decision maker's assumptions about what *stakeholders* believe, and how they expect stakeholders to behave in response to firm actions. It is hypothesized that this can result in different assumptions and expectations as to the long run financial benefits to the firm from CSR actions. Many of the benefits to firms from CSR (such as an increase in desirability to potential workers of socially responsible companies) depend upon the degree that people are cooperative and motivated by 'positive' other-regarding behavior and a sense of fairness. A firm leader who believes stakeholders are positively other-regarding will expect the firm to receive more benefits from proactive CSR investments than a firm leader who believes stakeholders are predominantly self-regarding. This result does not derive from a normative difference between the leaders but from a strategic one. The level of CSR investment often depends upon both, what the firm decision maker believes they should do (normative), and what they believe stakeholders will do based upon the resulting firm actions (strategic).

Chapter 4

OTHER-REGARDING BEHAVIOR: IS A MORAL COMPASS JUSTIFIED?

The significance of this distinction between the normative debate about goals and what leaders should do, and the strategic debate about CSR costs and benefits from differing beliefs and assumptions, begins to become apparent in an article by Waldman and Siegel [2008]. The article brings together two authors on the opposing sides of a variation of the debates described above. The article is organized as a sequence of four letters written back and forth between the two authors. The question debated is whether it is appropriate or inappropriate for top level managers within companies to incorporate their personal moral values into decisions concerning CSR. Siegel is "nervous" [Waldman and Siegel 2008, p. 118] when leaders make decisions partially directed by their moral beliefs due to his being, "a purist when it comes to the fiduciary responsibilities of top-level managers." He believes that decisions are more likely to be profit maximizing if they are made in the "cold and calculating" way described by Homo economicus. Waldman responds that there should be more concern with leaders who "lack a strong moral compass" [Waldman and Siegel 2008, p. 121]. In defense of this position, he suggests that the Sarbanes-Oxley legislation was, "necessitated by a system in which firms are remiss (or potentially remiss) in policing themselves in terms of social responsibility and ethical behavior" [Waldman and Siegel 2008, p. 122].

In examining the arguments of the authors, it is interesting to note that there seems to be a general agreement that leaders should make strategic, *profit conscious* decisions. In fact, Waldman agrees that leaders should *not* make investments in CSR that are clearly at the expense of profits. The main areas of contention seem to actually relate to, 1) the level of comfort with making investments in CSR that *may* improve profits in the long term but that are exceedingly difficult to quantify, and 2) differing views on the profitability impact of a morally guided, versus purely instrumental posture of the decision maker toward CSR. Siegel suggests that all CSR investments should be made *strategically* where, "The strategic use of CSR is defined as instances where there are *clear benefits* [emphasis added] to the firm for engaging in CSR" [Waldman and Siegel 2008, p. 119]. Waldman [Waldman and Siegel 2008, p. 120] counters that "Engaging in responsible actions only when the financial gain is clear may not always be the most prudent course of action":

> My real fear is that your insistence on such rigid instrumentality would preclude managers from taking initiatives, challenging the status quo, and working toward the new visions that, ironically, might help profit maximization in the long term. [Waldman and Siegel 2008, p. 120]

Ghoshal and Moran [1996] suggest that innovation related activities, such as RandD, are efficient only in the dynamic sense (i.e., in the long run). The same is likely true of corporate social responsibility (CSR) initiatives. McWilliams and Siegel [2000; 2001] demonstrate that corporate social performance and RandD are highly correlated. The direct benefits of individual initiatives in each realm are generally extremely difficult to determine up front, and often require intuition and foresight in making the investment decisions [Waldman and Siegel, 2008].

Waldman's arguments in favor of morally grounded leadership seems to be based less on the normative belief that it is the right thing to do (although this belief also seems evident), and more on the belief that being authentically responsible may, in aggregate, produce better financial performance in the long run. He suggests that Siegel's instrumental focus is representative of "transactional leadership" which focuses on exchange relationships, versus "transformational leadership" where a common sense of purpose and values inspires and opens the possibility for new visions. As evidence he describes a study that he co-authored which found that, "CEOs with strong economics values tended to be viewed by followers as highly authoritarian, while not being viewed as visionary" [Waldman and Siegel 2008, p. 123], and that these firms performed worse financially than firms run by CEOs with strong stakeholder values [who tended to be viewed as highly visionary]. He concludes that, "even though they pursue such an emphasis with profits squarely in mind, those profits may not be realized."

Waldman suggests that sometimes, "manager[s] fall back on logic and/or intuition" in making strategic decisions. Although Husted and Salazar [2006, p. 87] seem to subscribe more to Siegel's position, they acknowledge that, "Firms continue to invest in all sorts of projects, even though they may be uncertain about their ability to extract all the benefits provided by such investments. Strategic CSR investment is no different." Siegel then acknowledges that, as with RandD investment, there are instances where the long term benefits of CSR may be hard to identify beforehand such that, "perhaps a visionary leader can overcome this myopia" [Waldman and Siegel 2008, p. 124]. However, he also suggests that, "Until there is a larger body of empirical evidence in support of your assertion that "moral" leadership matters, I would be careful not to make bold predictions about the impacts of moral leadership on performance" [Waldman and Siegel 2008, p. 125].

THE IMPACT OF BEHAVIORAL ASSUMPTIONS ON STRATEGIC CSR

Consider, for example, the assumptions regarding human nature. As Herbert Simon observed, "Nothing is more fundamental in setting our research agenda and informing our research methods than our view of the nature of human beings whose behaviors we are studying...It makes a difference to research, but it also makes a difference to the proper design of... institutions: [1985: 293]". [Ghoshal 2005, p. 82]

The wide difference in beliefs between Waldman and Siegel as to the appropriate perspective for a firm decision maker to use provides a descriptive example of the potential impact of differing assumptions under the real world conditions of uncertainty, bounded rationality and selective perception. Although their debate seems initially to a normative one, the analysis of the arguments by each author uncovers that most of the real debate is between differences of opinion as to the potential benefits and costs *to the firm* of a decision maker using a moral compass in evaluating CSR investments. It is hypothesized here that a key issue underlying the stated differences between their beliefs and assumptions is the difference between their respective views about human behavior. More specifically, the key differences are proposed to relate to their beliefs about the degree to which people are self-regarding and self-interested versus cooperative, positively other regarding and social. It should be noted that the debate between Waldman and Siegel, and many of the examples in the current discussion, are related to issues that 'cross the moral/intrinsic versus neutral/instrumental divide.' However, the effect of recognizing uncertainty and differences in behavioral assumptions is still proposed to create a wide range of justifiable CSR investment levels even if a purely strategic perspective is taken.

The logic behind this proposition is based on the significant extent to which many of the benefits to the firm from CSR initiatives depends upon the degree to which people care about others, fairness, and desire for cooperative relationships with the company. For example, the degree of financial benefits a firm may get from instituting non-animal testing or dolphin free products, depends upon the degree to which customers and other stakeholders value the animals that are spared. Is it possible to develop cooperative relationships with government regulators and environmental NGO's, or are these relationships inevitably going to be based upon conflict? Much of the benefit to the firm from having a strong reputation for CSR in terms of, employee loyalty, productivity, and creativity, depends upon the degree to which employees care about making a contribution to the world and other intrinsic rewards, rather than only caring about their direct compensation and other extrinsic rewards.

Waldman et al. [2006, p. 1710] describe a consulting project where one of the authors witnesses the struggle of a CEO from a Fortune 500 company trying to rally his management team around, "a totally new conceptualization of the firm's strategy." When he was not achieving buy-in, the CEO organizes a three day retreat with the company's top 200 executives. After a morning of little progress selling the strategy, the CEO:

> ...changed gears and started talking about how the new strategy would help the company contribute to the global fight against AIDS......The impact of the five-minute talk about AIDS was eye opening. The mood of the group showed a discernable change. Managers started showing a stronger interest in the topic. [Waldman et al. 2006a, p. 1710]

Based upon the description of event, and the fact that the firm was not in the medical field, it seems that the shift in energy of the management team was likely much more based upon an authentic desire to be a part of contributing to the global fight against AIDS, than in an instrumental desire for financial success. Although this anecdote says nothing about the profitability of the strategy shift, it does highlight the desire of the management team to contribute to something beyond themselves, and beyond profits (altruistic preferences). It also demonstrates the potentially powerful motivating effect this has on their desire to make the strategy work:

Defined in terms of how the company will create value for society, purpose allows strategy to emerge from within the organization, from the energy and alignment created by that sense of purpose. [Ghoshal et al. 1999, p. 14]

The assumptions of human behavior behind this position are consistent with those of Stewardship Theory [Davis et al., 1997]. These authors describe employee by-in to the goals of the organization as "value commitment." They assert that value commitment can exist with a cooperative view of human nature, but "would not have economic utility and would not be a relevant part of the exchange agreement" using the standard economic assumptions of human behavior. The choice between developing relationships based upon self-interest (agency theory) or cooperation (stewardship theory):

.....is similar to the decision posed by a prisoner's dilemma....When both the principal and the manager choose a stewardship relationship, the result is a true principal-steward relationship that is designed to maximize the potential performance of the group....The psychological characteristics of each party predisposes each individual to make a particular choice. [Davis et al. 1997, p. 38]

Just like in the case of the prisoners' dilemma, this solution is not available with the assumptions of self-regarding agents. Although this description relates to the relationship between principals (owners) and agents (management), the conclusions seem to apply similarly to the approach taken toward relationships between company management and stakeholder groups. An emerging construct called "servant leadership" goes a step further by, "stressing personal integrity and serving other, including employees, customers, and communities" [Liden et al. 2008, p. 161].

Some believe the firm advantage from shared purpose described in the last example represents the primary advantage of the corporate form [Ghoshal and Moran, 1996]. This cooperative view of human behavior is diametrically opposed to the economic model of Homo economicus. Ferraro et al. [2005, p. 11] suggest that, "Self-interest forms the foundation for other fundamental premises in economics" and creates the focus on extrinsic incentives, the problems of agency theory and the prescriptions of transactions cost theory. For example, Williamson's [1981] transaction cost approach suggests monitoring and control to prevent opportunistic behavior is one of the main advantages of the firm. He suggests that both bounded rationality (resulting in incomplete contracting) and opportunism (resulting in the inability to extract reliable promises to act in a "stewardship fashion") must be prevalent for there to be a reason for the firm to exist on efficiency grounds. If one of these elements is missing then he suggests that the market could accommodate the other. In essence the firm exists to overcome the market failures caused by bounded rationality and opportunistic behavior. Hirshleifer [1994, p. 1] goes even further:

> Love and friendship may sustain cooperation among a few partners, but the elaborate division of labor essential for modern life has to rely on the force of self-interest. Pushing the point to an extreme, Hayek has contended that only when people learned to be selfish, learned to overcome their innate instincts toward communal sharing, did it become possible to make the transition from primitive society to free civilized life.

This view stands in sharp contrast to Cordes et al [2007] and Ghoshal and Moran [1996] who counter that focusing on monitoring and control can, in many cases, be counterproductive. Ghoshal [2005, p. 85] suggests that a 'positive' feedback loop can result where, "One of the likely consequences of eroding attitudes is a shift from consummate and voluntary cooperation to perfunctory compliance." This view has all been expressed by others [Cyert and March, 1992 [1963]; March and Simon, 1991; Jones, 1995]. Cordes et al. [2007] propose that corporate culture evolves in an evolutionary process similar to gene-culture co-evolution, where human predispositions toward cooperation and group-beneficial behaviors make the firm a suitable organizational to take advantage of these social predispositions.

Again, it appears that main differences between these views relate to differences in beliefs and assumptions of how people will behave. Williamson's view is grounded in an opportunistic version of Homo economicus. Cordes, Ghoshal, Davis and their colleagues seem to view human behavior to be, on average, far more cooperative than this. Although these authors acknowledge that opportunism does exist, and that people do act selfishly at times, they suggest a view of human behavior that ignores the cooperative, other-regarding portion of human behavior is likely to lead to inaccurate conclusions. With this perspective on human behavior it is more logical to devote resources to CSR. Jones [1995, p. 422] suggests:

> ...firms that contract (through their managers) with their stakeholders on the basis of mutual trust and cooperation will have a competitive advantage over firms that do not....The competitive advantage that accrues to moral firms takes the form of substantially increased eligibility to take part in certain types of economic relationships and transactions that will be unavailable to the opportunistic firms.

Long before the debate between Waldman and Siegel, Simon [1955, p. 99] suggested that the assumptions contained in economic man should be revised:

> Recent developments in economics, and particularly in the theory of the business firm, have raised great doubts as to whether this schematized model of economic man provides a suitable foundation on which to erect a theory -- whether it be a theory of how firms do behave, or of how they "should" rationally behave.

Although if asked further Siegel, and most other economists, would likely not suggest that the behavioral model of Homo economicus describes human behavior completely accurately. However, Siegel does seem to imply that the model provides a reasonable approximation for decision making related to CSR. Given this, it is not surprising that he sees little possibility that firms led by managers using a moral compass in decision making will produce better long run financial performance than firms led by managers using a purely instrumental, calculating perspective. A firm decision maker with a similar predominantly self-regarding view of human nature and behavior could be expected to agree. The suggestion by Waldman that thinking altruistically and strategically are not mutually exclusive seems to indicate that he views human behavior as more cooperative, other-regarding and social.

The main hypothesis here is that this difference in behavioral beliefs at least partially explains why Waldman advocates use of a moral compass for decision making, and that this view would likely produce a very different analysis concerning the costs, and particularly the benefits of investments in CSR. This difference in their respective beliefs around human behavior is also seen in their diametrically opposing reviews of another paper by Ghoshal [2005]. Waldman [Waldman and Siegel 2008, p. 122] states that he concurs with Ghoshal's conclusion that business schools, "propagating ideologically inspired amoral theories (that free) students from any sense of moral responsibility" may be contributors to the creation of business scandals such as that of Enron. Siegel [Waldman and Siegel 2008, p. 125], alternatively, concludes that Ghoshal's [2005] paper is a "slapdash, Pollyannaish essay" and that:

> ...perhaps we need *more* economics [which presents a "dismal" view of man] in MBA programs, not *less* economics, as Ghoshal advocates. I fail to see how a focus on "positive" outcomes or processes, as opposed to the "negative" view of economics, will result in better outcomes.

It is interesting to note that the educational backgrounds of the authors seem completely consistent with their views on this issue, and on human behavior in general. While Siegel has a PhD, a Master's and a BA in economics, Waldman has a PhD in Industrial and Organizational Psychology.

Different Shifts in the Strategic Benefits Curve

The framework by Husted and Salazar [2006] described earlier can be used to show conceptually how decision makers with different views of human behavior could come to very different conclusions on the strategically appropriate level of CSR investment. The key issue becomes, how much does the revenue benefit curve really shift in the long run? It is proposed that the evaluation of a decision maker that views human behavior as predominantly self-regarding and self-interested, will generally assume a smaller shift in the revenue benefit curve from CSR than someone who views human behavior as predominately cooperative, social and other-regarding.

For example, let's assume that the name of the hypothetical CEO who believes people are primarily self-interested and self-regarding is "H. Economicus." Another hypothetical CEO who believes human behavior is primarily cooperative, social and other-regarding is named "M. Compass." Now let's hypothesize about how each might evaluate the costs and benefits of a proposed CSR initiative that allows employees to volunteer during work time for one day a quarter. This scenario is depicted in figure 2 by the increase in social output from X_0 to X_1. We will assume that the cost in terms of lost work hours, any supplies, and cash funds the employer provides for the program will be the same in both cases, and result in the cost curve shifting up from C_1 to C_2. If H. Economicus is CEO, he or she might believe that the employees will view the experience as a nice change of pace and thus be more rested, resulting in a small productivity gain (effect a). In addition, the improvement in community relations and goodwill may result in a small increase in sales (effect d_{HE}). In total H. Economicus estimates that the Benefits Curve will shift upward from B_1 to B_{HE}.

If M. Compass is CEO, he or she might have a similar valuation of the productivity gain from the employees being more rested. However, given a view of people as significantly cooperative and other-regarding, M. Compass might expect a slightly larger revenue benefit due to the improvement in community relations from the program (d_{MC}). However, the biggest difference might relate to an impact on employees that H. Economicus does not expect. M. Compass may anticipate that many of the employees will find the experience immensely

than non-economics students. However, as noted by the authors, this difference could be largely the result of pre-existing characteristics of the individuals choosing to study economics, thus creating a 'self selection' effect, rather than the difference being the result of the training and exposure to the model of Homo economicus. To test for this causality, they conducted a separate survey experiment in which students from 3 introductory freshman classes (2 in microeconomics and one in astronomy) were asked four ethical dilemma questions, in both the beginning and end of the semester. The questions relate to whether, a) as a business person they would report a billing error that was in their favor, and b) whether they expect that others would, and c) whether they would return $100 lost by an identifiable stranger, and d) whether they expect that others would. Their results showed that students having taken just one semester of microeconomics at Cornell were more likely to become less honest over the semester than the students from the astronomy class who had not taken economics. Even the emphasis which the economics professor placed on the self-interest model seemed to impact the results, with the students from the class emphasizing the self-interest model more strongly showing a greater decline in both their own honesty, and the extent to which they expected others to be honest. The authors conclude that, taken together, these results suggest that exposure to the self-interest model from mainstream economic theory may reduce both a person's propensity to 1) behave cooperatively and honestly, and 2) to believe that others will behave cooperatively and honestly.

Although these results support condition two, the one identified study that finds economics students to be *more* honest than others was performed as a direct challenge to these results. Yezer et al. [1996] suggest that the non-economists in the ethics survey may simply have been more biased in answering the survey in 'the right way,' and that the economics students might simply be more honest as to what they would actually do if faced with the ethical dilemmas. To test this hypothesis, they created a real 'lost money experiment' based on the hypothetical lost money survey from Frank et al. [1993a]. They placed multiple envelopes with 10, $1 bills, and a note that the money was to repay a loan, on the floor of both economics and non-economics classes at George Washington University. As more letters dropped in economics classes were returned, they concluded that:

> The evidence in this paper implies that even if undergraduate students of economics display uncooperative behavior in specialized games or surveys, their "real-world" behavior is actually substantially more cooperative than that of their counterparts studying other subjects. [Yezer 1996, p. 177]

Although these results offer a reasonable challenge to the results of Frank et al. [1993a], Frank and Schulze [2000, p. 103] [1] note that, "while it is true that we are ultimately interested in real world behavior and experimental situations are different from them, results from 'real-world' observations are almost always open to conflicting interpretations as we cannot exclude influences other than those we want to test for." For example, they note that Yezer et al. [1996] could not control for gender, which has also been shown to be positively related to propensity to cooperate [Frank et al., 1993a; Selten and Ockenfels, 1998].

Despite the conflicting results from Yezer et al. [1996], the overwhelming evidence still seems to support the conclusion that those who study economics are, on average, less honest and cooperative than those who don't. From this, it seems reasonable to assert that students from economics may, on average, be less likely to view human behavior as cooperative, other-regarding and social than those from other disciplines. Frank et al. [1993a] find that if given an opportunity to make promises, economics students weren't significantly less likely to cooperate. This seems to suggest that much of the difference in propensity to cooperate found in the anonymous prisoners' dilemma games might have been more related to the students being less likely to expect others to cooperate, rather than being less likely to want to cooperate themselves [Frank and Schultze, 2000]. This interpretation supports the proposition that the behavioral beliefs are significant enough to influence *strategic* decision outcomes.

Although most studies reach a similar conclusion concerning the lower level of cooperative behavior of economics students, there is far less agreement as to the cause of that result. Some agree with Frank et al. [1993a] [2] that the education/indoctrination effect, likely related to the exposure to the self-interest model, is likely a significant contributor to this result [Boone et al.1999; Jones et al., 1990]. Some conclude that it is due more to a self selection effect, with those choosing economics being on average less cooperative and other-regarding before even taking the classes [Carter and Irons 1991; Frank and Schultz 2000; McCabe et al., 1991]. Even more conclude it is some combination of both, or don't explicitly conclude on this causality question [Marwell and Ames 1981; Kahneman et al., 1986a; Cadsby and Mayes 1998; Selten and Ockenfels 1998]. In aggregate, the evidence seems to at least somewhat support the assertion that exposure to the self-interest model impacts an individuals' behavioral assumptions in a way that reduces, both their propensity to cooperate, and their

---

[1] The author 'Frank' in this study [Bjorn] is different than the Frank [Robert] in Frank et al. [1993].

2 Although Frank et al. [1993] find evidence that the exposure to the self-interest model has a causal effect, they note that that evidence is "preliminary" and do not discount the possibility of a significant self selection effect.

propensity to expect others to cooperate. This seems like a conservative assessment of this evidence given that some scholars interpret it far more conclusively:

> The argument and empirical implications are straightforward: one effect of economics training is to strengthen beliefs in the pervasiveness, appropriateness, and desirability of self-interested behavior, which, in turn, should lead to exhibiting more self-interested behavior. [Ferraro et al. 2005, p. 14]

This interpretation could be made more conclusively had the self selection effect not received as much support in some studies. However, there is a case to be made for concluding that a considerable portion of any 'self selection' effect is still related to the individuals' beliefs about human behavior, and to their propensity to subscribe to the behavioral assumptions of Homo economicus. As suggested by Siebenhüner [2000], knowledge of the self-interest model as a widely subscribed to principal of the market economy is not the exclusive domain of those who have taken formal economics courses:

> The norm of self-interest is a case in point: It induces people to act publicly in ways that maximize their material interests, whether or not they are so inclined privately. This norm, like most other norms, reflects both a descriptive belief [people are self-interested] and a prescriptive belief [people ought to be self-interested]. [Miller 1999, p. 1056]

Miller and Ratner [1998, p. 60] conduct five studies that all show that people (mostly students) systematically overestimate the degree to which self-interest guides the behavior of others, even though it does not guide their own behavior to the same degree:

> The role of self-interest is not as great as many formal theories assume. Neither, it appears from the present research, is its role as great as laypersons assume.

Little direct evidence supporting or rejecting the third required condition of a causal relationship between a firm decision maker's behavioral assumptions (and thus propensity to see the value and possibility of cooperative solutions) and the level of CSR investment they choose to implement. However, the following is suggestive of such a possibility:

An Aspen Institute study [2001] found that student's values changed during their two years in the MBA program. Not surprisingly, over the time they were in business school, enhancing shareholder value became more important and customers and employees became less important for students. [Pfeffer 2005, p. 97]

Apparently something that was taught to the MBA students in this study supports the belief that enhancing shareholder value conflicts with enhancing customer and employee value. It does not seem to be a stretch to assert that a model of human behavior that created the prisoners' dilemma, and preaches the unavoidability of an uncooperative solution contributes to these and earlier reported experimental results with economics students. Although these comments are made concerning business education in general, there may be reason to believe that the effect will not be uniform among the different fields within business. In an examination of 200 US MBA programs, Evans et al. [2006] find that the relative size of the individual departments impacts the amount of ethics in the curriculum. Specifically, programs with relatively large marketing and management departments offer more required and elective ethics courses than programs with relatively more faculty in finance, economics and accounting. In line with the discussion here, they suggest that this may be significantly due to the behavioral assumptions underlying each discipline, with finance and economics focused on profit maximization and self-interested behavior while relatively more in marketing and management approach the issue from a sociological or psychological perspective.

Again, as suggested by Davis et al. [1997, p. 38], "The psychological characteristics of each party predisposes each individual to make a particular choice." There is evidence that such behavioral differences affect managers as well:

Using various managerial scenarios, Tetlock found that "managers of varying political persuasions subscribe to marketedly different assumptions about human nature that, in turn, shape their underlying philosophies of governance" [Tetlock, 2000: 320]. Differences in beliefs about human nature--that is, subjects' "ideological world view"--resulted in differences in how they reported they would manage people and organizations. [Ferraro et al. 2005, p. 15]

This is at best loosely suggestive of the asserted link between the view of human behavior embodied in firm decision makers, and their evaluations of choices concerning investment in CSR. However, the reasonably strong evidence suggesting that those who have studied [or even those who have chosen to study] economics are less likely to cooperate or expect others to cooperate, is the primary basis for the behavioral hypothesis discussed in this work. Based upon this theoretical argument, Manner (2009) uses KLD data (as a proxy for CSR) and a large sample of US firms and their CEO's to test whether there is a systematic difference in the level of CSR implemented by firms with CEOs having different undergraduate degrees. The results show that a firm's CEO having a bachelor's degree in economics is negatively and significantly related to strong/proactive CSP. The study also finds that the CEO having a bachelor's degree in humanities is positively and significantly related to strong/proactive CSP. No other undergraduate major showed significant results. These findings are consistent with the majority of the experimental results discussed in this section finding economics students less likely to cooperate and less likely to expect others to cooperate. They also represent preliminary evidence supporting the hypothesis that behavioral beliefs of the CEO impacts their analysis of CSR initiatives.

The results are significant despite the multiple decades of indoctrination into the 'norm of self interest' prevalent in the market economy. This suggests that if the results are from an economics indoctrination effect, there must be a strong 'path dependency' from the economics bachelor's education, that may create a filter [Hambrick and Mason, 1984] that biases everything that happens after. Boone et al. [1999, p. 347] site evidence that seems to add support for this possibility:

> Kuhlmann and Marshello [1975] demonstrated that individuals have tendencies to compete or cooperate in mixed-motive games where these tendencies – or orientations- are relatively stable.

To the extent that the results are based more on a self selection effect, it may be that the propensity to cooperate or not to cooperate is programmed into an individual's psychological make up at an even earlier age:

> Our beliefs about human nature help shape human nature itself. Our ideas about the limits of human potential mold what we aspire to become. They also shape what we teach our children, both at home and in the schools. [Frank 2004, p. 54]

SOCIAL NORMS AND FAIRNESS: INDIRECT COSTS FOR SOCIETAL LEGITIMACY

Management can continue down the well-worn path to illegitimacy or begin to chart a new course by laying claim to a higher purpose....Throw out the old paradigm while you still can, before the growing gap between companies' economic power and their social legitimacy proves right. Take responsibility before management is held to blame for stunting the growth potential of individuals, companies, and society. [Ghoshal 1999, p. 19]

As I read this quote today, it seems to contain a menacing foreshadowing of the global financial system crisis one decade later. Some would suggest that this crisis has been significantly caused by executives following the extremes of the 'norm of self interest' and not taking heed to the warning in this quote. The calls for general norms for responsible behavior have been discussed by many. Wood [1991, p. 699] suggests that, ".....businesses are not responsible for solving all social problems. They are, however, responsible for solving problems that they have caused, and they are responsible for helping to solve problems and social issues related to their business operations and interests" Kahneman et. al. [2001] note that actions that are both profitable in the short run and not obviously dishonest are sometimes perceived as unfair exploitations of market power, perhaps resulting in government regulations and/or the firm getting a reputation for unfairness. Corporations are not immune to social norms that are increasingly defining and demanding responsible [Epstein and Roy, 2001] and fair [Kahneman et al., 1986a] behavior, with punishment of violators common. Akerlof [2007] suggests that economic analysis based on traditional theory is often inaccurate because it misses the fact that people have norms for how they and others should behave.

Under this view, any costs incurred by corporations in satisfying societal norms and expectations could be viewed to reflect the 'societal legitimacy' cost of doing business. Although Jensen and Meckling [1976] may not subscribe to this view, their description of why agency costs are simply a part of doing business could be applied in an analogous way to social legitimacy costs [bracketed alternative phrases added]:

In conclusion, finding that agency costs [societal legitimacy costs] are non-zero (i.e., that there are costs associated with the separation of ownership and control in the corporation) [i.e., that there are costs associated with societal norms] and concluding there from that the agency relationship [the firm/society relationship] is non-optimal, wasteful or inefficient is equivalent in every sense to comparing a world in which iron ore is a scarce commodity (and therefore costly) to a world in which it is freely available at zero resource cost, and concluding that the first world is "non-optimal" - a perfect example of the fallacy criticized by Coase [1964] and what Demsetz [1969] characterizes as the "Nirvana" form of analysis.

The beliefs as to the level of societal norms required to achieve business legitimacy is likely to be significantly impacted by the beliefs about human behavior, with a person with a self-interested view estimating a lower level of norms than a person who views people as cooperative, social and caring about fairness. Kahneman et al. [1986b, p. S286] suggest that economic analysis based on the classical rationality assumptions explain away acts of caring and preferences for fairness, "…as isolated phenomena of little economic significance." From this belief, social norms for fairness will not be assumed to significantly impact the behavior of employees, customers and other stakeholders. The authors suggest that the significant experimental results demonstrating that people are often willing to do just that have profound implications for firms:

> A widespread readiness to resist unfair transactions or to punish unfair actors even at some cost could present a significant threat to firms in competitive environments [Kahneman et al. 1986b, p. S290].

They then go on to describe further experimental evidence that shows that a majority of individuals engaged in anonymous transactions are, "willing to incur a cost to reward fairness and to punish unfairness when the fair or unfair actions were directed at someone else" [Kahneman et al. 1986b, p. S291]. This situation is comparable to customers or employees that are willing to punish a company that does not treat *other* stakeholder groups in a manner that is perceived as fair.

Given the apparent expanding nature of the level of corporate social responsibility, a long term perspective seems to suggest the wisdom of an approach that expands CSR activities beyond those that seem clearly justified through explicit cost benefit analysis. Recognizing this dynamic creates even more uncertainty and variation in CSR investment levels that can be reasonably justified as in the long run financial best interest of a company:

> Long-term survival and profitability may, in these days of heightened awareness of the social impact of business, depend on farsighted social planning by business. [Klonoski 1991, p. 15]

When the implementation of CSR is determined using this long term perspective, the assumptions as to what responsibilities will be imposed on business in the future will have profound consequences for the actions justified by long term profit seeking. Issues such as public image, viability of the business system, avoidance of government regulations, can often be justified economically under this long run perspective guided by enlightened self-interest [Davis, 1973].

Chapter 6

WHY THE INTRINSIC TREATMENT OF STAKEHOLDERS MAY BE STRATEGIC

The foundation of a firm's activity is a new "moral contract" with employees and society, replacing paternalistic exploitation and value appropriation with employability and value creation in a relationship of shared destiny. [Ghoshal et al. 1999, p. 10]

Many of the assertions and discussions to this point use moral/intrinsic versus neutral/instrumental treatment of stakeholders to demonstrate how, depending upon their beliefs and assumptions of human behavior, different decision makers will often come to different conclusions concerning the strategic consequences of undertaking CSR related investments. However, the analysis holds even if the complexity of the normatively charged distinction between intrinsic and instrumental is not considered. In other words, the degree to which a decision maker believes people are self-interested versus cooperative, other-regarding and social is still asserted to impact the strategic level of CSR, even if a purely instrumental posture toward stakeholders is maintained. This section, however, will explicitly make the assertion that there may often be a reasonable argument to be made that an intrinsic treatment of stakeholders can actually be in the long run best interest of shareholders. It is asserted that whether investments made from that point of view will be evaluated as being visionary and financially profitable in the long run, or wasteful, depends significantly on the behavioral assumptions the decision maker uses to evaluate the costs and benefits of such investments.

INSTRUMENTAL IS ONLY STRATEGIC BY DEFINITION FOR ECONOMIC MAN

In the paper by Berman et. al [1999], the term instrumental as applied to the identification and treatment of stakeholders is effectively used interchangeably with the word strategic. Similarly, Husted and Salazar [2006, p. 84] state:

> Studies in the literature on instrumental stakeholder theory have also confirmed that a strategic approach to stakeholder management can have positive impacts on financial performance.

This prescription is grounded in the theory of the firm and the assumption that managers of publicly traded firms attempt to maximize profits *and* that a purely instrumental view of stakeholders and CSR initiatives is the way to achieve that goal [Waldman et al., 2006]. Although those arguing for an instrumental view of stakeholders typically equate this to *the* strategic view, it is asserted that this is an equality only when using assumptions that view human behavior as predominantly self-regarding and self-interested. However, if these assumptions are replaced with ones that view human behavior as significantly more cooperative, social and 'positively' other-regarding, then *the possibility* exists that an intrinsic view of stakeholders may paradoxically, at times, be the better strategic view:

> The difference between old and new is not just economic but also philosophical. In an organizational economy in which the essence of the company is value creation, the corporation and society are no longer in conflict. They are interdependent, and the starting point is a new moral contract between them. [Ghoshal et al., 1999, p. 13]

Freeman [1984] suggests that the paradigm assuming an inverse impact of ethical behavior and profits must change given the ability of stakeholders to impact profits in the increasingly complex economic activity of humans.

Although Husted and Salazar develop their argument to generally support a strategic [defined as instrumental] approach to decision making on CSR, they acknowledge that, "Altruistic decision making may also shift the benefit and cost curves in ways that may exceed the shifts from strategic decision-making" [Husted and Salazar 2006, p. 88]. Despite acknowledging this possibility, their definition of the altruistic firm as making CSR investment decisions with the goal of being "profit neutral," and suggesting these decisions are made without any strategic intent, effectively eliminates this possibility. However, as proposed by Waldman [Waldman and Siegel 2008], why can't a firm think "altruistically and strategically"?

THE EVOLUTION OF MORALITY: IMPLICATIONS FOR THE FIRM

Ones beliefs and assumptions concerning human behavior can have a particularly large impact on the perspective taken toward, and treatment of the employee stakeholder group. As discussed earlier, whether human behavior is seen as predominantly self-interested [or worse, opportunistic] or as cooperative, positively other-regarding and social, can significantly impact the belief as to the source of advantage the corporate form has over markets, and how this advantage can be cultivated. Wade [2007] suggests that human morality is part of an ongoing evolutionary process. Manner and Gowdy [2009] describe evidence that suggests that the human capacity for empathy evolved from primates. They demonstrate the feasibility of an evolutionary advantage for the group selection of positively other-regarding or moral behavior, if people have some degree of ability to identify those who are likely to cooperate. As described earlier, Cordes et al. [2007] propose that corporate culture evolves in an evolutionary process similar to gene-culture co-evolution, where human predispositions toward cooperation and group-beneficial behaviors make the firm a suitable organizational form to take advantage of these social predispositions:

> Given the previous argument that individuals whose moral sentiments are incompatible with the values of the firm's top management will tend to avoid, leave, or be driven out of the company and the argument that the moral sentiments of firm employees will be fairly well known, it follows that a firm will tend to have a relatively homogeneous culture with respect to morality. Thus, even though the behavior of corporations regarding moral issues will not be simple extensions of the morality of their top managers, firms will tend to be populated by employees whose moral sentiments are compatible with the values of their top management. [Jones 1995, p. 420]

Cordes et al. [2007] suggest that if a business leader focuses exclusively on profits [self-interest] they may, inadvertently guide the firm members to think selfishly and, paradoxically, not produce the desired profits. It is easy to see how this idea would be rejected by H. Economicus and accepted by M. Compass, resulting in significantly different assessments of the long run benefits of CSR in general, and to employee related CSR in particular.

SITUATIONAL MORALITY: IS IT POSSIBLE?

Some might suggest that the examples in the preceding section are not examples of intrinsic treatment of employees, but rather simply reflect enlightened instrumental treatment. For example, if the reason for allowing employees to volunteer on company time is simply because the decision maker anticipates a positive profitability impact, the act becomes simply another profit motivated, strategic decision made from an instrumental stance toward employees. Even Wood [1991, p. 711] suggests, "Motivations are not observable, and processes are observable only by inference." Actions taken by a firm motivated by an instrumental strategic view of stakeholders will, under some situations, seem effectively the same as the actions taken by a firm motivated by an intrinsic view of stakeholders [and will often be communicated as motivated by a morally grounded desire to be responsible].

This is likely one of the reasons why Siegel [Waldman and Siegel 2008, p. 125] is not inclined to make "bold predictions about the impacts of moral leadership on performance" and why economists focus much more on outcomes of behavior rather than on the motives behind these actions. However, it has been proposed by some, that it is virtually impossible to be 'situationally authentic'. Sen [1985] suggests that by relaxing "self-goal choice" [e.g., relaxing the focus on maximizing profit] by making commitment or justice the goal of decisions, cooperative [non-inferior] outcomes in prisoners dilemma situations can emerge. In this case, the Prisoners' Dilemma becomes an "assurance game." However, he suggests that the gains from cooperation cannot be fully exploited unless one adopts at the outset what everyone would call a *"genuinely unselfish"* point of view. By systematically picking the cooperative rather than self-interested choice they achieve the better equilibrium:

> If following such 'habitual' rules as opposed to relentless maximization according to one's goals, produces better results there will also be a "natural selection" argument in favor of such behavior modes, leading to survival and stability....If profits are a source of success, then a community with a value system that violates profit maximization [in this particular way] may become more successful and may come to dominate over other communities with profit maximizing value systems. [Sen 1985, p. 351]

For a firm to be viewed positively by employees, the investment community, government regulators and others that can affect the financial performance of the firm, it may often be that genuine [or intrinsic] value must be placed on stakeholders. An intrinsic façade that masks a calculating instrumentality may be seen through. An instrumental view of stakeholders applied decision by decision wouldn't transform the prisoners' dilemma into an assurance game as suggested by Sen [1985]. Frank [2004, p. 67] similarly suggests that a firm which systematically takes, "the morally preferred action….is better able than its opportunistic rivals to solve commitment problems that arise between owners, managers, and employees; it is better able to solve commitment problems that arise with customers."

This discussion does not prove that the degree of positive other-regarding behavior and preferences needed to make the intrinsic treatment of stakeholders strategically justifiable exists. The expected benefits described may be less than, equal to or greater than the costs of the intrinsic treatment. However, it does at least show why it is likely that decisions made using the behavioral model of Homo economicus would underestimate the benefits of an intrinsic approach.

Some of the empirical work exploring the instrumental versus intrinsic view of non-shareholder stakeholders has concluded that the instrumental view is both, representative of what firms actually do, and is more profitable [Berman et al., 1999; Hillman and Kiem, 2001]. Although these results seem to directly challenge the assertions in this section, it is important to recognize that this empirical work supporting the instrumental *view* focuses on *identification* of stakeholders exclusively, or treats identification of *who* to focus upon and *how* to treat the stakeholder groups identified as inseparable constructs. However, there does not seem to be a logical reason why an instrumental *identification* of shareholders necessarily requires an instrumental *treatment* of the identified stakeholders. The two issues seem to represent distinct constructs, as they represent distinct decisions by firm leaders. In addition, the definition of an instrumental stakeholder has been transformed in these analyses from, a) valuing the stakeholders' needs only as a means to profit rather than also as an ends in and of themselves, to b) a different criteria defining any stakeholder related to the company's core business as being instrumental. Although some would suggest that firms should focus on solving wide societal problems, the issues here relate to Wood's [1991] view that firms should focus on solving the problems that they create in the spirit of Waldman where they do so "strategically and altruistically" [Waldman and Siegel, 2008].

Chapter 7

CONCLUSION

The argument in this chapter, suggesting that treating stakeholders as having intrinsic value *may* be beneficial from a long term financial perspective, may or may not resonate. The purpose of the discussion is not to conclude upon this complex issue. The purpose is to raise the *possibility* that it might in some cases be true. Even without getting into a definitional debate about intrinsic versus instrumental, the discussion is at a minimum intended to highlight the often ignored issue of how uncertainty in determining the costs and benefits of proposed CSR investments often creates a wide range of justifiable investment levels in any given situation. Another goal is to suggest that a key factor influencing this variability in investment levels between decision makers, relates to their assumptions concerning human behavior. A decision maker that sees people as predominantly cooperative, 'positively' other-regarding and social will likely estimate a higher level of strategically appropriate CSR investment than someone who views people as predominantly self-interested.

Although this instrumental versus intrinsic, moral versus neutral debate is generally framed normatively, the discussion was meant to show that often the underlying debate is less a matter of different goals (profits or not), but rather a matter of different beliefs and assumptions concerning human behavior. If true, this has many implications for a society that seems to be moving toward more demands on business to engage in socially responsible behaviors. One implication relates to the educational content taught to economists and our future business leaders in general, and the models of human behavior used in particular. Although the other-regarding characteristics of humans are beginning to be incorporated in experimental and behavioral economic studies, they seem to have made less significant inroads into the educational content of economics and business school curriculums [Ghoshal, 2005]. A more realistic presentation of human behavior in these programs might go a long way toward addressing this issue. Siebenhüner [2000] suggests that the self-interest model is not the exclusive domain of those with formal economics or business educations. Although true, the negative relationship found by Manner (2009) between strong CSP and the CEO having a bachelor's degree in economics suggests that economics students seem to embrace this model more tightly than most.

Waldman [Waldman and Siegel, 2008] suggests that the potential problems of a purely instrumental treatment of stakeholders were seen in the accounting scandals that prompted the enactment of the Sarbanes-Oxley legislation. It can also be suggested that the financial crisis that has emerged in 2008 (and has now expanded in 2009) may be at least partially a consequence of a purely instrumental versus intrinsic treatment of stakeholders by the executives of the financial institutions involved. From news accounts it seems that many lenders treated less financially sophisticated potential mortgage clients and investors in mortgage backed securities in an instrumental [or perhaps even unethical] manner. Although it is unclear what regulations that will emerge from this crisis, it seems appropriate to suggest that, as with Sarbanes-Oxley, the regulations will be aimed at filling the void left by the lack of leaders using a moral compass to guide business decisions.

REFERENCES

Akerlof, G. A. [2007]. The Missing Motivation in Macroeconomics. *The American Economic Review, 97* [1], 5-36.

Andreoni, J. [1990]. Impure Altruism and Donations to Public Goods: A Theory of Warm-Glow Giving. *The Economic Journal, 100* [401], 464-477.

Berle, A. A., Means, G. C. [1933]. *The Modern Corporation and Private Property.* The MacMillan Company, New York 1933, Reprinted: William S. Hein and Co., Inc. Buffalo [2000].

Berman, S. L., Wicks, A. C., Kotha, S., Jones, T. M. [1999]. Does stakeholder orientation matter? The relationship between stakeholder management models and firm financial performance. *Academy of Management Journal, 42* [5], 488-506.

Bertrand, M., Schoar, A. [2003]. Managing with Style: The Effect of Managers on Firm Policies. *The Quarterly Journal of Economics, 68* [4], 1169-1210.

Boone, C., De Brabander, B., van Witteloostuijn, A. [1999]. The Impact of Personality on Behavior in Five Prisoner's Dilemma Games. *Journal of Economic Psychology, 20*, 343-377.

Cadsby, C. B., Maynes, E. [1998]. Choosing Between a Socially Efficient and Free-riding Equilibrium: Nurses versus Economics and Business Students. *Journal of Economic Behavior and Organization, 37*, 183-192.

Carroll, A. B. [1999]. Corporate Social Responsibility: Evolution of a Definitional Construct. *Business and Society, 38* [3], 268-295.

Carter, J. R., Irons, M. D. [1991]. Are Economists Different, and If So, Why? *Journal of Economic Perspectives, 5* [2], 171-177.

Cordes, C., Richerson, P. J., McElreath, R., Strimling, P. [2008]. A Naturalistic Approach to the Theory of the Firm: The Role of Cooperation and Cultural Evolution. *Journal of Economic Behavior and Organization*, forthcoming.

Cyert, R. M., March, J. G., 1963 [1992]. *A Behavioral Theory of the Firm.* Blackwell Publishers, Cambridge, Mass.

Davis, J. H., Schoorman, F., Donaldson, L. [1997]. Toward A Stewardship Theory of Management. *Academy of Management Review, 22* [1], 20-47.

Davis, K. [1973]. The Case for and against Business assumption of Social Responsibilities. *Academy of Management Journal, 16,* 312-322.

Dearborn, D. C., Simon, H. A. [1958]. Selective Perception: A Note on the Departmental Identification of Executives. *Sociometry, 21* [2], 140-144.

Enke, S. [1951]. On Maximizing Profits: A Distinction Between Chamberlin and Robinson. *The American Economic Review, 41* [4], 566-578.

Epstein, M. J., Roy, M. [2001]. Sustainability in Action: Identifying and Measuring the Key Performance Drivers. *Long Range Planning, 34,* 585-604.

Evans, J. M., Trevino, L. K., Weaver, G. R. [2006]. Who's in the Ethics Driver's Seat? Factors Influencing Ethics and the MBA Curriculum. *Academy of Management Learning and Education, 5* [3], 278-293.

Fehr, E., Fischbacher, U. [2003]. The nature of human altruism. *Nature, 425,* 785-791.

Fehr, E., Schmidt, K. [1999]. A Theory of Fairness, Competition, and Cooperation. *The Quarterly Journal of Economics, 114,* 817-868.

Ferraro, F., Pfeffer, J., Sutton, R. I. [2005]. Economics Language and Assumptions: How Theories Can Become Self-Fulfilling. *Academy of Management Review, 30* [1] 8-24.

Frank, B., Schultz, G. G., 2000. Does Economics Make Citizens Corrupt? *Journal of Economic Behavior and Organization, 43,* 101-113.

Frank, R. H. [1999]. *Luxury Fever: Money and Happiness in an Era of Excess.* Princeton University Press, Princeton and Oxford.

Frank, R. H. [2004]. *What Price the Moral High Ground?: Ethical Dilemmas in Competitive Environments,* Princeton University Press, Princeton.

Frank, R. H., Gilovich, T., Regan, D. T. [1993a]. Does Studying Economics Inhibit Cooperation? *Journal of Economic Perspectives, 7* [2], 159-171.

Frank, R., Gilovich, T., Regan, D.: [1993b], 'The evolution of one-shot cooperation', Ethology and Sociobiology 14, 247-256.

Freeman, E. R. [1984]. *Strategic Management: A Stakeholder Perspective.* Pitman Publishing Inc., Massachusetts and London.

Freeman, E. R., Liedtka, J. [1991]. Corporate Social Responsibility: A Critical Approach. *Business Horizons, July-August 1991,* 92-96.

Friedman, M. [1970]. The social responsibility of business is to increase its profits. *The New York Times, September 13,* 122-126.

Frye, M. B., Nelling, E., Webb, E. [2006]. Executive Compensation in Socially Responsible Firms. *Corporate Governance, 14* [5], 446-455.

Ghoshal, G., Bartlett, C. A., Moran, P. [1999]. A New Manifesto for Management. *Sloan Management Review, Spring 1999,* 9-20.

Ghoshal, S. [2005]. Bad Management Theories Are Destroying Good Management Practices. *Academy of Management Learning and Education, 4* [1], 75-91.

Ghoshal, S., Moran, P. [1996]. Bad For Practice: A Critique of the Transaction Cost Theory. *Academy of Management Review, 21* [1], 13-47.

Godfrey, P. C., Hatch, N. W. [2007]. Researching Corporate Social Responsibility: An Agenda for the 21st Century. *Journal of Business Ethics, 70,* 87-98.

Gowdy, J. [2005]. Corporate responsibility and economic theory: an anthropological perspective. *International Journal of Sustainable Development, 8* [4], 302-314.

Hambrick, D. C. [2007]. Upper Echelons Theory: An Update. *Academy of Management Review, 32* [2], 334-343.

Hambrick, D. C., Mason, P. A. [1984]. Upper Echelons: The Organization as a Reflection of Its Top Managers. *Academy of Management Review, 9,* 193-206.

Hamilton, W. [1964]. The general evolution of social behavior. *Journal of Theoretical Biology, 7,* 1-16.

Harbaugh, W., Mayr, U., Burghart, D. [2007]. Neural responses to taxation and voluntary giving reveal motives for charitable donations. *Science, 316,* 1622-1625.

Harrison, J. S., Freeman, E. R. [1999]. Stakeholders, social responsibility, and performance: Empirical evidence and theoretical perspectives. *Academy of Management Journal, 42* [5], 479-485.

Henrich, J. [2004]. Cultural group selection, coevolutionary processes and large-scale cooperation. *Journal of Economic Behavior and Organization, 53,* 3-35.

Hillman, A. J., Kiem, G. D. [2001]. Shareholder value, stakeholder management, and social issues: what's the bottom line? *Strategic Management Journal, 22,* 125-139.

Hirshleifer, J. [1994]. The Dark Side of the Force: Western Economic Association International 1993 Presidential Address. *Economic Inquiry, 32* [1], 1-10.

Husted, B. W., Salazar, J. [2006]. Taking Friedman Seriously: Maximizing Profits and Social Performance. *Journal of Management Studies, 43* [1], 75-91.

Jensen, M. C., Meckling, W. H. [1976]. Theory of the Firm: Managerial Behavior, Agency Costs and Ownership Structure. *Journal of Financial Economics, 3*, 305-360.

Jones, T. M. [1995]. Instrumental Stakeholder Theory: A Synthesis of Ethics and Economics. *Academy of Management Review, 20* [2], 404-437.

Jones, T. M., Thomas, T., Agle, B., Ehreth, J. [1990]. Graduate business education and the moral development of MBA students: Theory and preliminary results. Paper presented at the annual meeting to the International Association of Business and Society, San Diego, CA.

Kahneman, D., Knetsch, J. L., Thaler, R. H. [2001]. Fairness as a Constraint on Profit Seeking: Entitlements in the Market. *The American Economic Review, 76* [4], 728-741.

Kahneman, D., Knetsch, J. L., Thaler, R. H. [1986]. Fairness and the Assumptions of Economics. *Journal of Business, 59* [4], S285-S300.

Klonoski, R. J. [1991]. Foundational Considerations in the Corporate Social Responsibility Debate. *Business Horizons, July-August 1991*, 9-18.

Kolm, S., Ythier, J. [2006]. Introduction. In Elsevier B. V., *Handbook of the Economics of Giving, Altruism and Reciprocity Vol. 1.* Amsterdam, the Netherlands [ISSN: 1574-0714]

Kolstad, I. [2007]. Why Firms Should Not Always Maximize Profits. *Journal of Business Ethics, 76*, 137-145.

Liden, R. C., Wayne, S. J., Zhao, H., Henderson, D. [2008]. Servant Leadership: Development of a multidimensional measure and multi-level assessment. *Leadership Quarterly, 19*, 161-177.

Manner. M. H., Gowdy, J. [2008]. The Evolution of Social and Moral Behavior: Evolutionary Insights for Public Policy. *Ecological Economics*, Special Issue: Coevolution, forthcoming.

Manner, M. H., [2009], ' The Impact of Other-regarding Behavior and Bounded Rationality on Decision Making and Corporate Social Performance', Doctoral Dissertation, Rensselaer Polytechnic Institute, Troy, NY.

March, J. G., Simon, H. A. [1991]. *Organizations.* John Wiley and Sons, Inc. New York

Marwell, G., Ames, R. [1981]. Economists Free Ride, Does Anyone Else?: Experiments on the Provision of Public Goods, *Journal of Public Economics, 15* [3], 295-310.

McCabe, D. L., Dukerich, J. M., and Dutton, J. E. [1991]. Context, values and moral dilemmas: Comparing the choices of business and law school students. *Journal of Business Ethics, 10*, 951-960.

McGuire, J. B., Sundren, A., Schneeweis, T. [1988]. Corporate Social Responsibility and Firm Financial Performance. *Academy of Management Journal, 31* [4], 854-872.

McWilliams, A., Siegel, D. [2000]. Corporate social responsibility and Financial Performance: Correlation or Misspecification? *Strategic Management Journal, 21* [5], 603-609.

McWilliams, A., Siegel, D. [2001]. Corporate social responsibility: A theory of the firm perspective. *The Academy of Management Review, 26* [1], 117-127.

McWilliams, A., Siegel, D. S., Wright, P. M. [2006]. Corporate Social Responsibility: Strategic Implications. *Journal of Management Studies, 43* [1], 1-18.

Miller, D. [1988]. Altruism and the Welfare State. In Boulder and London, *Responsibility, Rights, and Welfare: The Theory of the Welfare State* [163-188]. Westview Press.

Miller, D. T. [1999]. The Norm of Self-Interest. *American Psychologist, 54* [12], 1053-1060.

Miller, D. T., Ratner, R. K., 1998. The Disparity Between the Actual and Assumed Power of Self-Interest. *Journal of Personality and Social Psychology, 74* [1], 53-62.

Mitchell, R. K., Agle, B. R., Wood, D. J. [1997]. Toward a theory of stakeholder identification and salience: Defining the principle of who and what really counts. *Academy of Management Review, 22* [4], 853-886.

Myers, D. G. [1993]. *Who is Happy and Why?* Avon Books. New York.

Orlitzky, M. [2008]. Corporate Social Performance and Financial Performance: A Research Synthesis. In Oxford University Press, *The Oxford Handbook of Corporate Social Responsibility* [113-136], Oxford.

Orlitzky, M., Schmidt, F. L., Rynes, S. L. [2003]. Corporate Social and Financial Performance: A Meta-analysis. *Organization Studies, 24* [3], 403-441.

Panapanaan, V. M., Linnanen, L., Karvonen, Mi., Phan, V. T. [2003]. Roadmapping Corporate Social Responsibility in Finnish Companies. *Journal of Business Ethics, 44*, 133-148.

Pfeffer, J. [2005]. Why Do Bad Management Theories Persist? A Comment on Ghoshal. *Academy of Management Learning and Education, 4* [1], 96-100.

Post, S. [2005]. Altruism, happiness, and health: It's good to be good. *International Journal of Behavioral Medicine, 12*, 66-77.

Samuelson, P. A. [1993]. Altruism as a Problem Involving Group versus Individual Selection in Economics and Biology. *AEA Papers and Proceedings, 83* [2], 143-148.

Schwartz, C., Meisenhelder, J., Ma, Y., Reed, G. [2003]. Altruistic social behaviors are associated with better mental health. *Psychosomatic Medicine, 65,* 778-785.

Selten, R., Ockenfels, A. [1998]. An experimental solidarity game. *Journal of Economic Behavior and Organization, 34,* 517-539.

Sen A. [1985]. Goals, Commitment, and Identity. *Journal of Law, Economics, and Organization, 1* [2], 351-355.

Shrivastava, P. [1995]. The role of corporations in achieving ecological sustainability. *Academy of Management Review, 20,* 936-960.

Siebenhüner, B. [2000]. Homo sustinens-- towards a new conception of humans for the science of sustainability. *Ecological Economics, 32,* 15-25.

Simon, H. A. [1955]. A Behavioral Model of Rational Choice. *The Quarterly Journal of Economics, 69* [1], 99-118.

Simon, H. A. [1979]. Rational Decision Making in Business Organizations. *The American Economic Review, 69* [4], 493-513.

Simon, H. A. [1987]. Satisficing. *New Palgrave Dictionary of Economics* 4, 243-244. Macmillan and Company, London.

Thomas, A. S., Simerly, R. L. [1994]. The Chief Executive Officer and Corporate Social Performance: An Interdisciplinary Examination. *Journal of Business Ethics, 13* [12], 959-968.

Trivers, R. [1971]. Evolution of reciprocal altruism. *Quarterly Review of Biology, 46,* 35.

Vogel, D. [2005]. *The Market for Virtue: The Potential and Limits of Corporate Social Responsibility.* R. R. Donnelley, Harrisonburg, Virginia.

Waddock, S. A., Bodwell, C., Graves, S. B. [2002]. Responsibility: The new business imperative. *Academy of Management Executive, 16* [2] 132-148.

Waddock, S. A., Graves, S. B. [1997]. The Corporate Social Performance - Financial Performance Link. *Strategic Management Journal, 18* [4], 303-319.

Wade, N. [2007]. Scientist finds the beginnings of morality in primate behavior. *New York Times.* Late Edition [East Coast], New York, N.Y. March 20, 2007. pg. F.3

Waldman, D. A., Siegel, D. S. [2008]. Defining the socially responsible leader. *The Leadership Quarterly,* 19, 117-131.

Waldman, D. A., Siegel, D. S., Javidan, M. [2006]. Components of CEO Transformational Leadership and Corporate Social Responsibility. *Journal of Management Studies, 43* [8], 1703-1725.

Williamson, O., E. [1981]. The Modern Corporation: Origins, Evolution, Attributes. *Journal of Economic Literature, 19* [4], 1537-1568.

Wood, D. J. [1991]. Corporate Social Performance Revisited. *Academy of Management Review, 16* [4], 691-718.

Wright, P., Ferris, S. P. [1997]. Agency Conflict and Corporate Strategy: The Effect of Divestment on Corporate Value. *Strategic Management Journal, 18*, 77-83.

Yezer, A. M., Goldfarb, R. S., Poppen, P. J. [1996]. Does Studying Economics Discourage Cooperation? Watch What We Do, Not What We Say or How We Play. *Journal of Economic Perspectives, 10* [1], 177-186.

Zamagni, S. [1995]. Introduction. In Edward Elgar Publishing Limited, *The Economics of Altruism*. Hants, England/Vermont, USA.

Reviewed by: Gowdy, J.
Professor of Economics and Rittenhouse Chair
Rensselaer Polytechnic Institute

Reviewed by: Baron, R. A.
Bruggeman Professor of Entrepreneurship, Lally School of Management
Rensselaer Polytechnic Institute

INDEX

58

Index